"Rules of the Game"

For

LIFE

COLLEGE

HIGH SCHOOL

Discussion Guide

For

Parents, Teachers and Youth Leaders

HARVEY J. COLEMAN

Coleman Management Consultants, Inc.

authorHOUSE®

AuthorHouse™
1663 Liberty Drive
Bloomington, IN 47403
www.authorhouse.com
Phone: 1-800-839-8640

First published by AuthorHouse 4/4/2011

ISBN: 978-1-4567-4412-0 (e)
ISBN: 978-1-4567-4413-7 (sc)

Library of Congress Control Number: 2011902754

Printed in the United States of America

Preface

The information in the book "Rules of the Game for High School, College, Life" is very powerful and can be life changing for many. To help young people process the information and utilize it to its fullest, some discussions with adults may be helpful. Whether it is parents with their children, teachers with their students, youth leaders with their charges or leaders of book clubs, the guide will allow an adult to lead meaningful discussions with young people and allow them to work through many of the challenges they are confronted with in today's competitive world.

The questions are listed by chapter so that each chapter can be addressed and understood before advancing to the next topic. Of course, our questions are by far not the only ones that should be presented. You may think of many more that better address the specifics you might want to share with the young person or people with whom you are in discussion. The same is true with our suggested "possible responses." In preparing for your discussions take time to think about the other responses that could be made or that you want to share.

Most people want to move beyond the theory of the "rules" and try to determine if they really apply to their lives. For this reason, any personal examples you can share as the discussion leader will make the information they read in the book much more interesting and believable.

There are no definitive correct answers for any question. The right answer is in the "eye of the beholder" which will be based on their life objectives and values. It is good to remind the group that when making choices in life, only they (as an individual) determine whether their choices are good or bad for they are the ones who have to live with the consequences of them.

As parents, mentors, and counselors we know we can only offer advice, every young person must make the decisions that will mold their lives.

Let's help them all we can.

Table of Contents

I. **Overview**
    A. Each chapter has a brief overview to remind you of the content.
    B. Discussion Questions
        *   A series of suggested questions is provided for each chapter along with some possible responses you might expect to hear from young adults.
    C. Responses to Share
        *   These responses are provided to help you as a discussion leader to share perspectives that might not have been considered. They are by no means a complete list but are given to trigger some personal thoughts you may want to share with an individual or a group you are facilitating. This is a great time to tap into your personal life experiences. People like the transition from theory to actual events.
    D. Chapter Summary
        *   At the end of each chapter is a section where all the major points of each chapter are put into bullet point form for your quick reference.

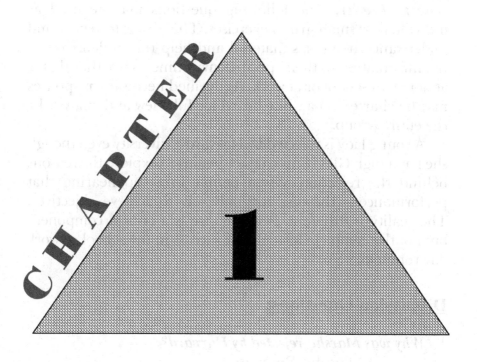

CHAPTER

1

The People Game

Overview:

Note to Leader: The following questions may be used as individual or small group exercises. The idea is to review and understand the book's material and help the students relate the information to their specific environments whether that is at home, in school or at work. As deemed necessary, responses may be charted on a white board for full view and analysis by the entire group.

A young lady is rejected by Harvard University even though she has a high GPA. This chapter begins to explore the reasons behind the rejection. Often people grow up hearing that performance is the one and only way to achieve objectives. The reality is different. Performance is a critical component but not the complete formula for success in the school or work environment.

Discussion Questions:

1. *Why was Marsha rejected by Harvard?*
    A. Possible Responses:
        i. Grade point average was not high enough.
        ii. The school had a quota to take minority students.
        iii. Her high school was rated low.
    B. Responses to Share:
        i. Premier schools not only expect a high grade point average but also expect applicants to show leadership and well

roundedness. Some areas that might have helped her include:

ii. Participation in student government.
iii. Participation in extracurricular activities – such as:
    A. Sports teams;
    B. Band, cheerleading;
    C. Clubs such as: drama, science, debate, library, language, etc.;
    D. Activities outside of school such as: Jr. Achievement, Boy/Girl Scouts, church groups, etc.;
    E. Holding leadership positions in clubs or organizations;
    F. Receiving awards;
    G. Life experiences such as: trips, foreign exchange programs, camps, etc.

2. *"The game is about people." List all of the ways people can help you now and in the future?*
    A. Possible Responses:
        i. Hiring…give you a job;
        ii. Writing letters of recommendation;
        iii. Providing financial aid;
        iv. Teaching new skills;
        v. Giving advice and support.

3. *How much control do you have over your destiny? Why?*
    A. Possible Responses:
        i. None…everyone tells you what you will do.
        ii. Only a little.
    B. Responses to Share:
        i. You have full control of your destiny.
        ii. You have and will continue to make choices in your life.

      iii. Parental guidance may be a strong influence on your choices.

      iv. The following exercise is to be done in pairs. In pairs, make notes and discuss the responses. Ask volunteers to share with the full group. Take about 10 minutes for the activity: ***Name one choice you have made in your life that you regret. Why do you regret it? Now name one choice you have made in your life that made you happy. Why did it make you happy?***

4. ***Who are the most influential people in your life today?***
   A. Possible Responses:
      i. Parents
      ii. Teachers
      iii. Close friends
      iv. Relatives
      v. Religious leaders
      vi. General friends/classmates
   B. Responses to Share:
      i. Good suggestions!
      ii. It might seem we will never leave any of these people. However, as we get older those who make up this influential group will be replaced by others.

5. ***Who are people in the future who might help you?***
   A. Possible Responses:
      i. Teachers
      ii. Principal
      iii. School counselors
      iv. Religious leaders
      v. Community and political leaders
      vi. Family friends

B. Responses to Share:
    i.   Again, a great list.
    ii. You may also want to consider that people you work with (colleagues, supervisor) may be of assistance.
    iii. Don't forget about your classmates! You never know where a classmate might connect in their life and have the ability to help you!

6. *What are some major choices you have already made in your life and/or must make in the near future?*
    A. Possible Responses:
        i.   Activities to join;
        ii. The major to select in school;
        iii. The personal image I want;
        iv. Schools to consider attending;
        v.   To join a fraternity/sorority and which one;
        vi. How hard to study.
    B. Responses to Share:
        i.   You can see that there are many, many choices you will make all of the time for every aspect of your life!

Key Points:

*   Everything that happens involves people.
*   You have full control of your own destiny.
*   It is necessary to make continuous choices.
*   Success involves more than good grades.
*   Everyone has a choice of moves in the game of life.

Chapter One Summary

<u>*The People Game*</u>

- Marsha even with a high grade point average is rejected by Harvard. She learns that grade point averages are important but is only one of the items premier schools require.

- Life is a game, the game is about people everything else is detail. All decisions that will affect your life will come from parents, teachers, professors, employers. Learn how to be effective with all of them.

- In the definition of "a game" it must include a contest or a struggle, it must be competitive and it must give every participant choices. These are all the elements we face in the game of life.

- We have control of our lives through the choices we make.

- Many people succeed in life because they are willing to make difficult choices. These difficult choices are often referred to as "paying your dues." An example would be to attend college or not.

- No matter how difficult a situation, you always have a choice.

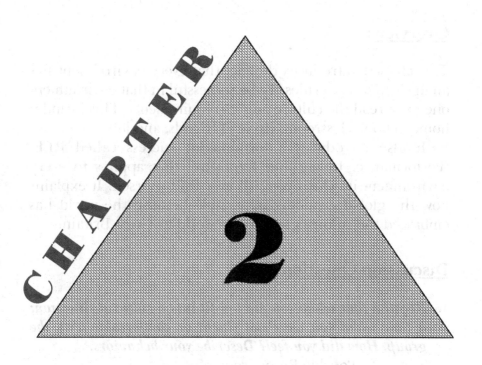

CHAPTER

2

Reading the Environment

Overview:

This chapter introduces the fact that every environment has an unwritten set of rules. To be successful in that environment one must read the culture and its requirements. This includes home, school, classroom, circle of friends, and job.

It also introduces a formula for success called P.I.E. (Performance, Image and Exposure) that applies to every environment in which you will ever find yourself. It explains how the global economy is possible because the world has embraced the culture given to the world by Great Britain.

Discussion Questions:

1. *Recall a time when you did not fit into a cultural situation; a time when you were not fluent or comfortable with the group. How did you feel? Describe your behaviors.*
   - A. Possible Responses:
       - i.   Uncomfortable.
       - ii. Out of place.
       - iii. Not smart.
       - iv. Awkward.
       - v.   Self conscious.
   - B. Responses to Share:
       - i.   Thanks for your thoughts. Most likely the group reaction also caught your attention. Often in these types of situations

the members of the group attempt to make you more comfortable and only succeed in putting you in the spotlight. This is the reason that when we know ahead of time where we are going that we attempt to learn something about the event or activity as well as the people who will attend. This adds to our personal comfort level.

ii. Mr. Coleman refers to this as "reading the environment" in his book. Without knowing what we are doing we attempt to figure out how to be successful in all of our environments.

iii. **Question for the group:** Describe success in High School? In College? (You may want to chart the responses). For high school it might include: being popular, having a high grade point average, being in the top 10% academically, being respected by students and teachers, making athletic teams, becoming a student leader, etc. for college they may say: adapting well while being away from home, being accepted into the fraternity/ sorority of choice, becoming a student leader, etc.

iv. **Next question for the group:** What are the success factors that everyone must follow to be successful in High School or College? (List the group contribution). *Possible Responses:* get good grades, follow procedures, ask questions, use good study habits, be serious about the courses, have and show a positive attitude, get to class on time, participate in student government, activities, and athletics.

2. ***Reviewing the success factors listed, which ones have you chosen to aggressively do well?***
   A. Possible Responses:
      i.   Get to class on time
      ii. Do homework.
      iii. Participate in activities.

3. ***Identify which success factors your close social circle of friends feel are important. Which ones do they avoid?***
   A. Responses to Share:
      i. This will vary according to the specific networks that each student belongs to...generally what will happen is that "likeminded" people hang out with "likeminded" people. As a student, it is important to recognize how influential our group of friends and associates are at various times in our lives. If you are constantly around people who do not think that studying is important, then you might not think that studying is important. If you hang out with people who enjoy getting good grades, then you are more likely to follow that pattern.

4. ***What is your reaction to learning that success is based upon P.I.E. and the weight of Performance is 10%; Image is 30%; and Exposure is 60%? In your opinion is this fair or unfair; logical or illogical?***
   A. Possible Responses:
      i. Their responses are most likely going to be extremely varied. Frequently, the weighting is unfair and illogical in the minds of people. This is mainly due to the fact that everything that has been taught up to this point has focused on "performing well." Students should be

encouraged to openly discuss the P.I.E. formula and understand clearly how it is to be interpreted.

ii. The weighting does not have anything to do with the amount of effort or time spent in each area. Each student needs to understand that they should give maximum effort to performance but also to image and exposure as well.

Key Points:

- Reading the environment is a skill.
- The rules are made by those at the top of the pyramid.
- Rules apply in every environment.
- The whole world plays by the same rules.
- Performance, Image, and Exposure are the elements of success.

Chapter Two Summary

<u>*Reading The Environment*</u>

- To be successful in any environment, it is important to know the written rules (policies and practices) but also understand and adhere to the "unwritten rules" (tradition and culture) as well.

- In reading the rules in any environment, one should observe, question, interpret and then adapt.

- Adapting is the most difficult of the four steps because it often requires a person to change themselves to fit.

- Rules allow all environments to function properly and orderly whether it is high schools, colleges, companies or even the global economy.

- One of the unwritten rules state that whoever is at the top of any pyramid has the right to make the rules. When the British Empire ruled the world they created the rules that govern the global economy today.

- Becoming fluent in any language allows you to fit and operate effectively within that culture. Fluency in a culture takes two to three years.

- The game board of life has seven levels. Each level has a culture or language of its own. In order to be sponsored into the next higher level, a player must show that they can comfortably fit with the people and activities of that level.

- The interview process is a chance to show that you do fit into the next higher level.

- Every time you interface with another person you can leave either a negative or positive impression.

- The formula for success lies in three major areas. Performance, Image and Exposure. All three are essential but have different weights.

    - Performance   10%
    - Image   30%
    - Exposure   60%

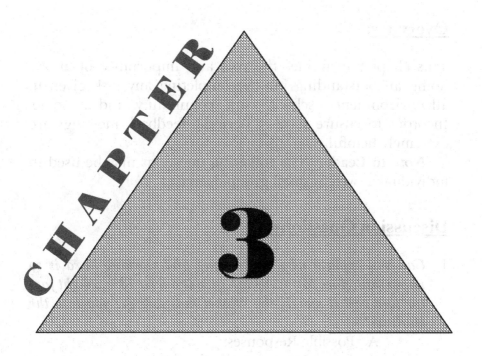

CHAPTER 3

Performance – The Entry Ticket

Overview:

This chapter examines the role and importance of always doing an outstanding job by completing any task given in all environments...school, work, community, and at home. In order to ensure success, periodic feedback meetings are extremely helpful.

Note to Leader: The following questions may be used in individual as well as small group exercises.

Discussion Questions:

1. *Can you explain why, if studying and working hard is so important, does Mr. Coleman give it only a 10% weight factor and call it merely the "ticket that will get you into the stadium?"*

    A. Possible Responses:
        i.   It is not really that important.
        ii. Everyone knows to work hard so everyone is doing the same thing.
        iii. It depends on the subject area.
    B. Responses to Share:
        i.   All good and competitive students study hard and get good grades. This makes good grades a "given" or merely a starting point for competition to begin.
        ii. It is expected from everyone and thus

16

diminishes in importance when judging students.

2. *If you are struggling in a subject area, what are the things you should consider doing to correct the situation?*
    A. Possible Responses:
        i.   Get a tutor.
        ii. Work harder and longer.
    B. Responses to Share:
        i.   Study harder.
        ii. Learn better study habits.
        iii. Give that subject more attention.
        iv. Ask for help from other students, teachers or your parents.

3. *In submitting all written materials to your teacher or professors, what are the things you must consider to maximize your grade?*
    – Possible Responses:
        i.   Understand the assignment.
        ii. Are certain of the expectations.
        iii. Meet all required criteria.
        iv. Are clear on the required format.
        v.   Know the grading standards.
        vi. Ensure correct spelling and grammar.
        vii. Always meet announced deadlines.

4. *When you feel a grade that has been given to you is wrong, what should you do?*
    A. Go and talk to the teacher or professor but before you do make sure:
        i.   You check all your facts.
        ii. You have prepared a logical case...emotions do not help in disputes.
        iii. You go into the discussion with a positive attitude.
        iv. Your demeanor is polite and respectful.

    B. Ask how you can improve on your next assignment. This will indicate that you want to improve.

5. ***What is your reaction when you are told you could do better or are doing something wrong?***
    A. Possible Responses:
       i. I feel that people are talking down to me.
       ii. I feel that I am not perfect.
       iii. I think that some people have standards that are too high.
       iv. I feel people are trying to show how little I know and how much they know.
       v. I know people are trying to help me and I should listen.
       vi. I feel like a failure.
    B. Responses to Share:
       i. Understand that constructive feedback is an opportunity to learn how to do better.
       ii. Listening carefully will allow people to see that you are seriously trying to improve.
       iii. There are people who really want to see you succeed.
       iv. Everyone needs feedback to grow.

Key Points:

- In order to get to the top you must deliver first-class performance.
- It is essential to understand the task requested.
- Periodic feedback meetings help you accomplish your tasks.
- Performance is based on subjective and objective standards.
- Doing an outstanding job all of the time is essential to success.

Chapter Three Summary

Performance – The Entry Ticket

- Although performance is weighted as 10%, good performance is essential to even be considered for promotion. All of your good competitors will be good performers.

- Performance is a given…it merely gets you into the competition.

- No person is irreplaceable no matter how good their performance may be.

- With summer jobs, part-time employment or intern programs, take charge of your performance evaluations:

    - Know what your boss expects of you and write it down in a plan.
    - Review that plan with your boss and get agreement.
    - Have periodic meetings with your boss to review your progress and accomplishments.
    - Make sure all work you do is to the best of your ability.

- At appraisal time, make sure you have prepared your case to ensure the highest possible rating.

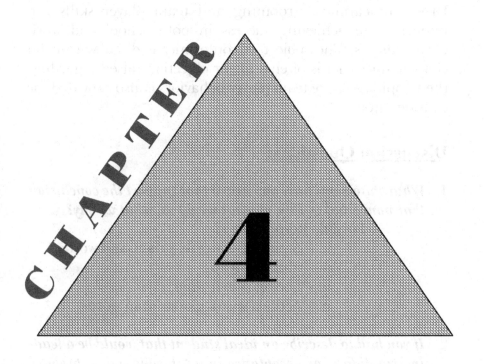

Image

Overview:

Dress, appearance, grooming and team player skills are important in achieving success in both school and work environments. The subject of conformity is discussed in the chapter since that is often a major objection raised regarding these topics. A list of team player behaviors is also provided for consideration.

Discussion Questions:

1. *What statements have you heard that support the conclusion that nonverbal is 70% of what we do vs. what we say?*
   - Possible Responses:
        i. "A picture is worth a thousand words."
        ii. "Talk is cheap."
        iii. "Seeing is believing."
        iv. "Actions speak louder than words."

2. *If you had to describe an ideal student that would be a leading candidate for acceptance in a top college or a premier company, what traits would they possess?*
   A. Possible Responses:
        i. High grade point average.
        ii. Student leader.
        iii. Volunteers for community work.
        iv. Positive attitude.
        v. Conservative image.
            1. No visible tattoos.
            2. No trendy or unique haircuts.

3. No piercings.
4. Conservative dress and
appearance.
vi. Good communication skills.
vii. Polite disposition.
viii. Does not use slang when talking.
ix. Participant in school activities.
B. **Note**: When the list is complete, have students review each trait and classify them as Performance,
Image or Exposure. They will note that high
grades are important but there are many other
factors that make a strong candidate.

3. *What are some of the ways we use nonverbal communications?*
– Possible Responses:
i. To reinforce or complement our verbal
messages such as:
1. Saying "come here" and also us-
ing hand gestures
2. Head nod while saying "yes"
ii. As a substitute for words like:
1. Ok
2. Come here
3. Go back
iii. To emphasize our words by:
1. Pounding fist on a desk while
talking
2. Pointing while say "over there"
iv. To regulate our interactions by:
1. Looking at a clock or watch
2. Turning away from the speaker
3. Standing if speaker is sitting
v. To contradict our verbal message such as:
1. Gesturing "come here" while ver-
balizing "stop"

4. **What are some of the ways we transmit nonverbal messages?**

    – Possible Responses:

        i. Through facial expressions such as:
            1. Eyes
            2. Eyebrows
            3. Mouth
            4. Forehead

       ii. With silence

      iii. With gestures like:
            1. Body movements
            2. Hands
            3. Head nodding
            4. Hand to face

       iv. Through time/timing as with:
            1. Sense of time
            2. Use of pauses in speech
            3. Regard for others' time

       v. Touching by:
            1. Hugging
            2. Arm on/around shoulder

       vi. Walking

      vii. Body Posture like:
            1. Angled or frontal direction
            2. Weight evenly distributed

      viii. Space needs such as:
            1. Distance someone sits or talks to us
            2. Personal space

       ix. Office space indicators like
            1. Size of desk
            2. Type of desk
            3. Bookcases
            4. Square footage
            5. Doors
            6. Windows
            7. Pictures

8. Chairs
9. Tables
10. Carpeting

x. Cubicle workspace
1. Size
2. Number of cabinets
3. Location on the floor
4. Usable work space
5. Height of panels

xi. Appearance factors such as:
1. Dress
2. Weight
3. Grooming
4. Social graces (manners)

xii. Tone of voice may indicate:
1. Sarcasm
2. Helpfulness
3. Anger, annoyance
4. Confidence
5. Disgust

Note: *As an exercise, put the students in small groups and have them select one of the areas and provide examples of how messages may be communicated. For fun, have students demonstrate some facial and body nonverbal movements.*

Some rules of nonverbal communication to share:

A. We are always communicating.
B. Nonverbal is the most credible channel of communication.
C. We believe nonverbal messages more than verbal messages.
D. Nonverbal behaviors should never be interpreted out of the context of an interaction.

Also keep these things in mind in relationship to dress.

     A. Look in your mirror several times before you leave home.
     B. If you are not sure something matches...it doesn't
     C. If you don't like how you look before you leave the house, it won't get better.
     D. Bring the positive attitude to school or work; leave the other one at home.
     E. Dress each day as if you might interact with the most important people in your school or work environment.

Appearance, Dress and Grooming

Background:

Acceptable appearance, dress and grooming standards have changed in the last several years. Many environments have adopted casual styles. It is important for you to understand the written and unwritten standards applicable in any environment where you wish to be successful. Personal appearance and grooming choices communicate a great deal about you as a student or a professional. Business casual or simply casual does not equate to sloppy, unkempt or "at home" casual dress.

Dress style and mindset go hand in hand. Think about the times when you dressed up for an activity, your posture and walk may have changed. Now, recall a time when you dressed very casually, again your walk, posture, and mannerisms may have changed.

Each time you get dressed; think about what you want your appearance to communicate to others about you. Select appropriate items from your wardrobe to communicate messages such as:

• Confidence	• Focused
•ᵻ In Control	• Determined
• Knowledgeable	• Sophisticated
• Serious	• Approachable

Remember that a positive attitude is also part of your appearance. As students you may have or get part-time jobs, summer jobs or become interns with an organization and if uniforms are not provided you will need to decide the messages you want to communicate through your dress and grooming choices. Here is a worksheet to provide some guidance in this area.

<u>Worksheet:</u>

Review each item listed below and identify standards you believe are acceptable for men and women in a school or work environment. Please be specific. After identifying various standards, determine whether you believe the standard is Rewarded (R) – meaning the standard makes a positive statement or whether it is simply Tolerated (T) – meaning the standard is not completely acceptable but will be allowed in the environment.

1. Clothing	12. Decorated nails, toes
2. Hairstyle/haircut	13. Uniforms
3. Jewelry	14. Personal grooming
4. Makeup	15. Shirts (with or without collars)
5. Weight	
6. Greetings	16. Blouses (various necklines, materials)
7. Visible tattoos	
8. Body piercings	17. Jeans
9. Speech	18. Fashionable.fad clothing
10. Facial hair	19. Shoes
11. Leg & footwear	20. Decorated teeth

Exercise: Have students describe the proper and important dress they are seeing in their current environments.

Key Points

- Like-minded people tend to associate as friends.
- A team player attitude moves individuals closer toward success.
- Nonverbal behaviors communicate more than words.
- Everyone conforms to something!
- Dress, general appearance, grooming and behaviors communicate messages to others all of the time.

Chapter Four Summary

Image

- Image has a weighting of 30% as a success factor. It includes your dress, speech, attitude, demeanor and every other area of your personal expression.

- 70% of all of our communications come in the area of non-verbal messages.

- Nonverbal communication is our first language. Speech is the second language learned.

- Dress and personal grooming is a powerful way we share our mindset with others. Always send messages that will allow you to reach your personal goals.

- Always remember you cannot not communicate. Everything you do or choose not to do, will tell people who you are at any given time.

- Social networks (FaceBook, Twitter and MySpace) are fun but must be monitored carefully. Many people who make decisions about your life have access to your various sites. Always put your best foot forward.

- Everyone conforms to one culture or another. Even when you do not conform you are conforming to the non-conforming culture. Chose the conformity that will best allow you to reach your goals.

- Culture and fads should not be confused. Cultures extend from generation to generation. Fads are fleeting, from a few months to a few years. Cultural values are much more lasting.

Having a team attitude is one of the most important image messages that can be sent. They include such things as:

- Desire to participate
- Willingness to take risks for the team
- Willingness to be flexible
- A problem-solver focus
- Always willing to help
- Wanting the team to succeed

• People who don't have the same goals as you will often try to discourage you from reaching yours. This could even include family and friends. Have the courage to withstand those who are not supportive.

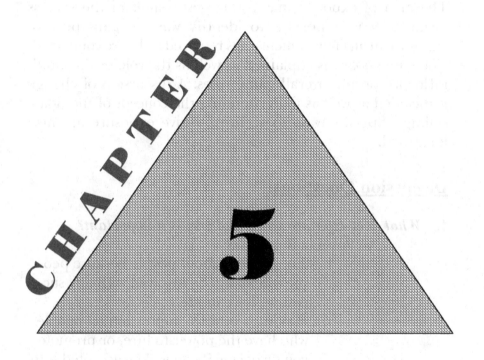

CHAPTER

5

Exposure

Overview:

The area of exposure has the largest weight in the success formula. It is important to identify ways to gain positive exposure in all environments ...as required tasks are completed. The game board is explained as well as the role of England's influence on the overall game rules. A discussion of change is included as well as understanding the concept of the "glass ceiling". Specific ways to secure positive exposure are also identified.

Discussion Questions:

1. *What does exposure mean and why is it important?*
   A. Possible Responses:
      i. The game is about people because people will always be involved with any success we have in life.
      ii. Making a positive impression on people who have the power to hire, or promote you or decide if you will be accepted into their college or university.
      iii. Positively influencing people who will serve as your references for school or work opportunities.

2. *What is a sponsor and how does sponsorship work?*
   A. Possible Responses:
      i. A sponsor is someone who has the decision power to make a difference in

someone's life. A person will sponsor someone they know, have interacted with or have seen them interact with others. If impressed, he/she may decide to support the person in their career aspirations.

ii. If a person is sponsored, their success or failure will have a direct effect on how others see the sponsor's abilities to evaluate talent or potential.

iii. It is crucial to be seen by others in a positive light.

3. ***List some activities in high school or college that will give you opportunities to gain positive exposure:***
   A. Possible Responses:
      i. Run for student government – you will become known even if you do not win.
      ii. Join and participate in clubs and school organizations.
      iii. Participate in athletics and extra curricular activities.
      iv. Get involved in community activities.
      v. Join a fraternity or sorority.
      vi. Learn new skills.
      vii. Broaden your personal networks.

4. ***Give some examples of "whoever is at the top of any pyramid has the right to make the rules".***
   A. Possible Responses:
      i. Parents for the home.
      ii. Teacher for the classroom.
      iii. Principal for a school.
      iv. General for an army.
      v. Pope for Catholics.
      vi. Chairman for a Company.

5. ***When England was an empire (The British Empire) they were at the top of the world's pyramid. What influence has England left on the world today?***

    A. Possible Responses:

        i. Democracy.

        ii. Two houses of government.

        iii. The English language.

        iv. Social Activities: golf, tennis, sailing, polo among others.

        v. Trial by your peers.

        vi. The socio-economic class structure.

6. ***There are seven (7) different class levels and we are all born into one of them. Is it possible for anyone to change class levels in their lifetime? What is needed to change levels?***

    A. Possible Responses:

        i. Yes, a person can change class levels.

        ii. First a personal desire to change levels is necessary.

        iii. Improve educational status (additional degrees).

        iv. Learn the lifestyle activities of the desired class level.

        v. Connect with a sponsor.

7. ***Change can be very emotional and difficult. What are some of the barriers that prevent people from changing?***

    A. Possible Responses:

        i. Haven't decided what they want in life.

        ii. Change makes people uncomfortable. It forces them out of their comfort zones.

        iii. Learning new things makes people feel and look stupid.

        iv. Learning new things causes separation from current friends and family.

        v. Uncertain of acceptance into new circles.

        vi. People feel they have the right to be themselves and don't want to conform.

        vii. Changing lifestyles could force a change in values, which is difficult.

8. ***What does hitting a "glass ceiling" mean and when does it happen?***
   - A. Possible Responses:
     - i. When advancement in a career or life stops.
     - ii. It generally occurs whenever a person chooses not to learn the next higher life-style activities.
     - iii. It also happens when a sponsor is not found.

9. ***What major changes have you made in your lives that are/ were different from your parents?***
   - A. Learned various sports activities.
   - B. Joined clubs and/or organizations.
   - C. Participated in cultural activities different from my own.
   - D. Learned to use computers and the internet.
   - E. Actively met and engage with a wider variety of people.
   - F. Looked for and accept travel opportunities and/ or programs.

<u>Key Points:</u>

- Who you know and who knows you is critical to success.
- It is important to get positive exposure inside and outside of your valued environments.
- Change, if constant, leads to growth.
- Understanding how the system works is necessary for success.
- Mentors and sponsors are needed to succeed.

Chapter Five Summary

Exposure

- Everything you accomplish in life will be with the help of people. Grades, hiring, promotions, assignments, raises all will be connected to people. Letting people know who you are and what you want to accomplish will allow the people who can help...to help.

- If in a job, ways to gain positive exposure:

    - Volunteer for internal projects.
    - Assume more responsibility within a specific job function.
    - Get involved in the community.
    - Participate in company sponsored activities.
    - Keep abreast of "state of the art" techniques.
    - Visibly demonstrate a team player attitude.
    - Be willing to learn new skills and experience different situations.

- In high school or college, ways to gain positive exposure:

    - Run for student government.
    - Join clubs and school organizations.
    - Participate on athletic teams.
    - Get involved in community activities.
    - Join fraternities and sororities.
    - Continually learn new lifestyle skills.

- England's influence on the "game rules" is very evident. They gave the world golf, tennis, sailing, polo, democracy, trial by jury, two houses of legislature, language and many more things.

- They also gave the world the socio-economic class structure. We are all born into one of those classes. This is where we start the game as individuals.

- To move from one level to the next a person must adapt the language, values and lifestyle of the next upper level. Everyone must decide if the change is worth the reward.

- Once you show you can fit into the next level, you will be sponsored to that level and be given the financial resources to live at that level.

- Hitting a "glass ceiling" usually occurs when a person refuses to adapt to the next higher level. "When you are through changing, you are through" being competitive. This, of course does not define happiness. Not moving to the next level may be the best choice for many people.

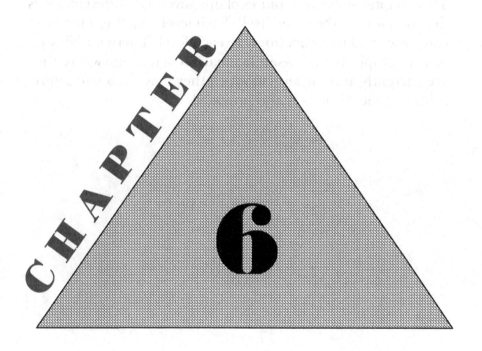

The Game Board

Summary:

This chapter identifies and explains seven (7) different levels (leagues) within the game itself. Each level contains a list of 12 categories and how they apply to each level. There is a lifestyle activity graph that allows individuals to determine where they are currently and the level to which they may choose to aspire. A list of general rules is also provided.

LIFESTYLE ACTIVITIES

Categories	One	Two	Three	Four	Five	Six	Seven
Socio-economic Class Titles	Drop-out Class	Next-to-bottom, Welfare, Poverty Class	Labor Class, Lower–Middle, Blue Collar, Working Class	Standard–Middle, Suburban–Middle, White Collar, Professional, Managerial	High Level, Upper Middle Class	Next-to-top, Celebrity, Nouveau Riche, Lower–Upper, Jet Set	Elite, Top, Upper–Upper, Aristocratic, Governing, Old Money
Education	1–2 Years of High School	Possibly High School Degree	Usually High School Degree	Commercial, Associate Degree, Technical and Junior College Degree	College Degree, Solid Schools	Advanced Degree, Better Schools	Advanced Degree, Best Schools, Boarding/Prep Schools
Occupation	Out of Work	Part-time Worker at Minimum Wage	Non-exempt Manual Administrative Workers	Exempt, Accountants, Programmers, Sales Reps, Managers	Middle Management, Small Business Owners, Airline Pilots, Medical Professionals	Regional Politicians, Top Corporate Execs, Movie, T.V., Sports Personalities	Family Business, National Politics, Wall Street Lawyers, Top 20 Banks
Organizations and Clubs	Church Club	Y.M.C.A./Y.W.C.A. Boys/Girls Clubs, Church-Related Clubs	Moose Club, Eagle Lodge, Cultural Clubs, Gun Clubs	Mason, Rotary, Non-profit, Civic Organizations	Neighborhood Country Clubs, Swim/Tennis Clubs	Regional Country Clubs, Local Community and Boards	Exclusive National Social Clubs, Profit & Non-profit National Boards
Social Activities	Church-Related	T.V., Church	Movies, Hunting, Fishing, Camping, Family Activities, Bowling	Entry Level, Theater, Tennis, Golf	More Accomplished in Sports and Cultural Events, Entry Level Skiing & Bridge	Sailing, Skiing, Flying, Charity Drives	Yachting, Horse Breeding, Patron Fine Arts, Fox Hunting, Polo
Location and Type of House	Housing Projects, Inner City, Homeless	Housing Projects, Inner City, Rent Subsidized	Urban Areas, Own Mobile Home, Ethnic Committees	Own Homes in Suburban Communities, Tract Houses	Country Club Communities, In-town Renovations	Extra Large Homes, Custom Built, Tennis Court, Pool	Mansions, Multiple Homes

LIFESTYLE ACTIVITIES (continued)

Categories	One	Two	Three	Four	Five	Six	Seven
Entertaining in the Home	Rarely Entertain	Extended Family Members, Holidays	Family & Friends, Barbecues, Casual	Social Cocktail Parties, Self Prepared, Sporty	Cocktail Parties, Business & Social, Catered, Dressy	Dinner Parties Business & Social, Catered, Dressy	Dinner Parties, Very Political, Extravagant, Formal
Earning Power	None	$8,000–$35,000	$12,000–$75,000	$18,000–$250,000	$100,000–$500,000	$250,000–Millions and above	Millions, Inherited Wealth
Other Investments	None	None	Savings Series "E" Bonds, Lottery Tickets	Inner City Condo IRAs, C.D.s, Treasury Bonds	Vacation Home, Investment Portfolio	Limited/General Partnership, Revenue Producing Properties	Stock Ownership, Interlocking Directories
Fine Arts	Never Attend Theater	Rarely Attend Theater	Attend Popular Theater Productions	Mainly Theater, Some Ballet, Opera, Symphony, Museum	Season Tickets, Ballet, Opera, Symphony, Museum	Serve on Fine Arts Committees & Boards	Patron of the Fine Arts
Car	No Car	1 Used Car	Intermediate Used, Pick-up Truck	Big American Car, 1 Other Used Car	Mercedes, Cadillac, Other Luxury Cars	Rolls Royce, Bentley, Multiple Cars	Chauffeur Driven Limousine
Vacation Activities	None	Home to Parents	1 Week Family Vacation, Home to Parents	1 Week Shore, Mountains, 1 Week, Home to Parents	U.S.A. Vacation, Cruises, Shore, Mountains	Exclusive Resorts Abroad Once a Year	Most Exclusive Resorts, Extended Vacation Abroad, Seasonal Homes
Committees & Boards	Not Involved	Involved in Church Work	Non-Profit Volunteer Work in Ethnic Community	On Committees of Mainstream Non-Profit Organizations	Chair Committees of Major Non-Profit Organizations	On Boards: Non-Profit Regional Corporation, Local Arts	Chair Boards of National Non-Profit Major Corp., Fine Arts

Discussion Questions:

1. *Looking at the grid, determine the level where your parents were when you grew up. Discuss the various categories.*

2. *Again, looking at the grid, identify the lifestyle you would like to obtain before your life is over.*

3. *Here is a Summary of the Rules:*
    A. Every person is born into a class level. This is the lifestyle achieved by your parents at the time of your birth.
    B. Jobs in organizations and small businesses correspond to the socio-economic class levels. Each job, from entry level to executive management will fit into the structure. No level is better or worse than any other. The key is to live at the level that makes you happy.
    C. Money is not the sole criterion of level acceptance. You can't buy class, or the ability to execute a given language or a promotion.
    D. An individual must be introduced and sponsored into the next level. People do things for others with whom they are comfortable. It is necessary for an individual to demonstrate capabilities of functioning at a higher level or league.
    E. Leagues are possessive of their members. Once a comfort level is established, individuals do not want to lose members of their group (this includes friends, neighbors, work associates and sometimes even family).
    F. Once entrance to a league is gained, the means to function at that level will be provided. Raises are given in organizations, contracts are awarded to businesses, and financial deals are shared with friends.

G. People do not necessarily want a title....they want a lifestyle. Although titles are important and valued, the ability to live a specific lifestyle tends to be more important.

H. Whoever is at the top of a pyramid has the right and obligation to make the rules. Systems and organizations must have rules to prevent chaos and anarchy.

I. When you're through changing, you are through. Change is a fact of life. Self-improvement and personal growth have long been associated with success.

J. Execution is the name of the game. Understanding what is required is not enough. An individual, to be successful, must effectively use all acquired skills and knowledge.

Key Points:

- The game board contains seven (7) levels/leagues spread across 12 lifestyle activities. Rules govern the lifestyle activities levels/leagues.
- No one activity will define who you are, however, your overall lifestyle will.

Chapter Six Summary

The Game Board

- This chapter can best be viewed by reviewing the game board described on pages 122 and 123.
- Some general thoughts to be considered about the dynamics of the game board:
    - There are seven levels on the game board. Organizational America starts at level three.
    - We are all born into one of these seven leagues.
    - The areas of lifestyle include:
        1. Occupation
        2. Where people live
        3. Locations of home
        4. Entertaining in the home
        5. Money
        6. Educational level
        7. Leisure activities
        8. Fine arts
        9. Cars
        10. Vacation choices
        11. Organizations and clubs
        12. Community involvement
    - Jobs in organizations and small businesses correspond to socio-economic class levels.
    - An individual must be introduced and sponsored into the next level.
    - Leagues are possessive of their members.
    - Whoever is at the top of any pyramid has the right to make the rules.
    - Execution is the name of the game.

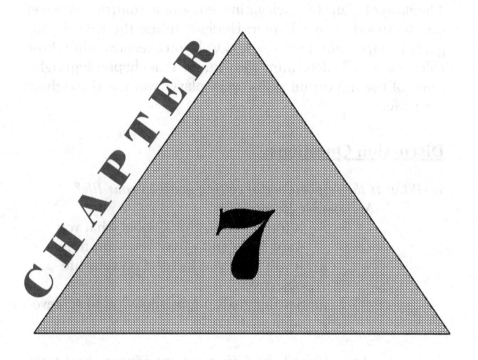

CHAPTER

7

Game Skills

Overview:

The skills of planning, delegating, emotional control and power are discussed in the chapter. Understanding the rules in any game is important; however, how well you execute within those rules will usually determine the winner. This chapter highlights some of the important skills every player will use throughout their life.

Discussion Questions:

1. *What is the importance of setting goals in your life?*
   A. Possible Responses:
      i.   It forces you to think about what you want to do and where you want to go.
      ii. It will keep you focused on your life objectives.
      iii. Setting goals might allow you to achieve your goals faster.

2. *Think about, identify and discuss some of your short-term, mid-term and long-term goals.*
   A. Possible Responses:
      i.   Get to the next grade.
      ii. Graduate from High School.
      iii. Get into the college I want.
      iv. Get a job.
      v.   Learn a new skill or activity.

3. ***What do you believe will be some of your most difficult obstacles which will keep you from reaching your objectives?***
    A. Possible Responses:
        i. Not enough time.
        ii. Social and sports activities.
        iii. Not studying hard enough.

4. ***What are some possible negative consequences when you don't control your emotions?***
    A. Possible Responses:
        i. It keeps you from thinking clearly.
        ii. You might say or do things you will regret later.
        iii. You might lose the respect of others.
        iv. People might not want to be around you.
        v. You might worry too much.

5. ***Have you ever lost your temper? What was the result?***
    A. Possible Responses:
        i. An argument.
        ii. A lot of confusion.
        iii. No resolution.
        iv. Loss of friendship.

6. ***What are some things you can do to prevent losing your temper?***
    A. Know yourself: Understand the things that make you angry and try to work on eliminating those "hot buttons".
    B. Get family members and friends to point out to you when you let your emotions take control.
    C. Listen to what people say and don't take everything personally.
    D. When you are angry, take some time and think before you respond.

Planning: An Exercise ----

    A. Using one of your short, mid or long term goals:
        i. Identify every obstacle that might keep you from reaching that goal.
        ii. Think of a solution that will help you overcome each obstacle.
        iii. Set time frames to implement your solutions.
    B. Let the group define **POWER**: The definition of power is "the ability to influence a situation." Another term for power could be leadership.

7. *What are some ways you can gain more influence at school?*
    – Possible Responses:
        i. Assuming a leadership role in the organizations and clubs you join.
        ii. Help other people.
        iii. Become visible in a positive way.
        iv. Learn as much as you can on all subjects – "knowledge is power."
        v. Create a personal image that is respected and rewarded in your environment. What are some of the characteristics of that image? Make a list.
        vi. Associate with other people who have influence.

Key Points:

- Goal setting is an important skill.
- Successful people control their personal emotions.
- Power is the ability to influence others.
- It is important to understand how to get, use and keep power.

51

Chapter Seven Summary

Game Skills

- As with any game, the ability to master the basic skills will usually allow you to play that game more effectively.

- The most critical skills include goal setting, emotional control, delegation and planning.

- **Goal Setting**
    - Without goals, you can easily travel in directions that are not of true interest. Truly if you don't know where you're going you could end up somewhere else.
    - Goals should be set in long term, mid-term and immediate timeframes.
    - In setting goals talk to people, try new things and always have fun on your journey.

- **Emotional control**
    - Losing emotional control does not help in any competitive situation. A player must keep their wits about them to make sound decisions.
    - Points to consider to control one's emotions:
      1. Be open to other opinions.
      2. Be an active listener. Try to understand what people are really thinking and saying.
      3. Don't take everything personally.
      4. Remember, everyone has a right to their opinion, even when it doesn't agree with yours.
      5. Remember, whoever is at the top has the right to make the rules.

- **Delegation**
  - This skill might apply later in your career but should be mastered as soon as possible.
  - People at the top must learn to delegate to free themselves to think strategically .
  - Delegating does not make you lazy it merely frees you up to take on other activities.

- **Planning**
  - In reaching your objectives, it is realistic to think there will be obstacles. Planning allows you to anticipate those obstacles and to put solutions in place to avoid or overcome them before they happen.
  - Planning allows you to test your strategic thinking and problem solving skills.

- **Gaining Power (Influence)**
  - Power is mainly gained by practicing the rules of Performance, Image, and Exposure (P.I.E.). All three are methods of growing your influence in any environment.
  - Power should always be used for the good of the organization and not for personal gain.

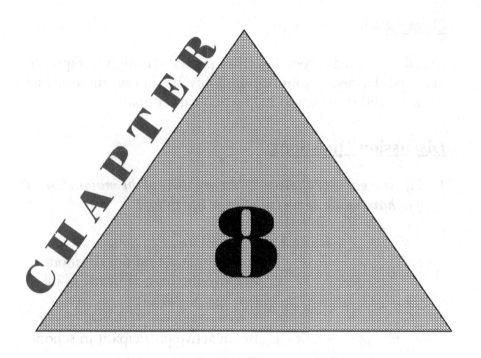

CHAPTER

8

Why Are the Rules Important?

Overview:

In order to reach career objectives career planning is required. Personal choices are your responsibility. It is important to attract mentors and sponsors to help reach career goals.

Discussion Questions:

1. *Life is a game of choices. What are some of the major choices you have made concerning your life so far?*
    A. Possible Responses:
        i. In High School to...
            1. Stay in school and not drop out.
            2. Achieve the highest grade point average possible.
            3. Take college prep courses or not.
            4. Be an active participant in school activities.
            5. Decide which college to attend.
            6. Follow the advice of parents, teachers, and counselors or not.
        ii. In College....
            1. Choose a fraternity or sorority to join.
            2. How hard to study and/or party.
            3. Selecting a major.

4. Attend graduate school or get a job first.
5. Apply for internship programs and which ones.
6. The company to join as an employee.

2. ***What are the steps I can take to change levels/lifestyles by learning new activities?***
   A. Possible Responses:
      i.   Talk with people who have changed lifestyles.
      ii. Associate with people who engage in the activities you want to learn.
      iii. Identify the activities you would like to learn.

Key Points:

* In order to be successful you need to know the rules.
* Career planning is helpful to reach goals and objectives.
* It is important to have mentors.
* Making choices is your responsibility.

Chapter Eight Summary

<u>*Why Are The Rules Important?*</u>

• All environments must have rules. To not have rules would create chaos, anarchy and disorder.

• The better you understand the rules of your environments, the more effective you will be.

• It is important to become a mentor to others by sharing the rules you have learned with peers and younger people.

• Remember these rules do not just apply to you, your school, your company or even this nation, but the entire global economy. To understand the rules allows you to better understand what is going on in the world.

• Also remember you are in the game right now. Every choice you make will have some impact on you and your future.

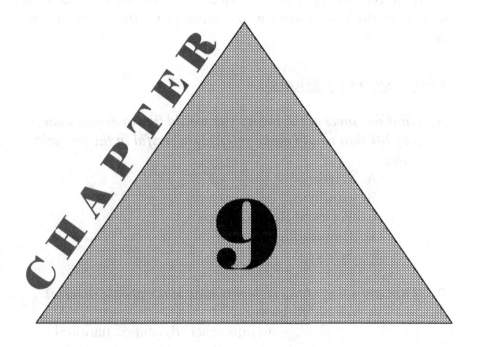

CHAPTER 9

The Challenge

Overview:

Each individual must define success for themselves. In this diverse world it is important to understand differences among people.

Discussion Questions:

A. *What are some of the things you would like to accomplish in your life that would make you feel successful in the following areas:*
    A. Career
    B. Family
    C. Personal Relationships
    D. Community
    E. School

B. *What are some of the elements that make people diverse?*
    – Possible Responses:
        i. Age, gender, race, disability, national origin, sexual orientation, personality, language, values, socio-economic levels among other things.

C. *Why is it important to understand differences among people?*
    – Possible Responses:
        i. To be more effective in all environments in which we live, work and socialize.

ii. To better understand what is going on in the United States and the World.

Key Points:

* Success is personally defined.
* Understanding people and their differences will make you more successful in a diverse world.

Chapter Nine Summary

<u>*The Challenge*</u>

- The game is about people, and in today's society people are very diverse. Learning about and accepting people differences is a powerful asset to any player.

- Success is always defined by you as an individual. Everyone does not want the same things out of life.

- You are the CEO of your life. The sooner you develop a life financial plan the better.

- Knowledge is power. The more you learn about the game and its requirements the less chance you will become a "victim of the system."

- When in problem or challenging situations, try to always think outside the box. Trying new solutions might be the most effective way to solve those situations.

- Remember, you are in control. You will make the decisions that will define your life. Also remember to constantly learn new things, keep growing yourself and when you set an objective in life…just do it. Remember it's a game.

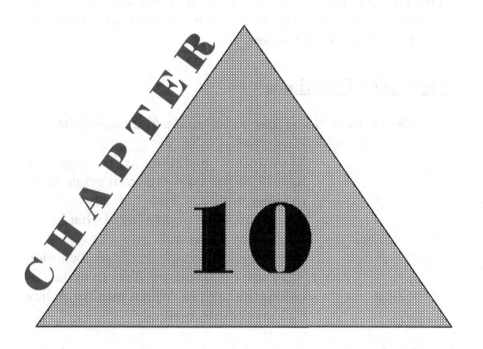

CHAPTER

10

Rules of the Game

Overview:

This chapter summarizes many of the historical "unwritten" rules that have been shared throughout the book. They are listed in a quick read fashion.

Discussion Questions:

1. *What are the "unwritten rules" and why do they exist?*
   – Possible Responses:
      i. They are the quotations and sayings that have been passed down from generation to generation.
      ii. They exist to let people know what it takes to be successful.
      iii. They establish socially acceptable behavior.
      iv. They are the standards used to make decisions but are not written into the policy and procedures manuals.

2. *Are there any rules listed in Chapter 10 that you do not understand?*
   – Possible responses should be dealt with as they arise.

3. *What are some sayings (or rules) you have heard from your parents, teachers, or other sources that are not listed in the book?*
   – Possible responses should be recorded and discussed as contributions are made.

4. ***If I change myself, am I "selling out"?***
    – Possible responses:
        i. Yes, you should be true to yourself.
    – Response to Share:
        i. Change is a fundamental requirement of life. As you accept new challenges and environments, adapting to those new environments will require change. Do not fear change…embrace it.
        ii. The world is changing too rapidly for anyone to be effective and remain stagnate. "When you are through changing… you are through."

5. ***What well known celebrities/athletes who are very talented, who have recently been in the news and dropped in prestige because of a negative image or because of negative exposure due to their behavior(s)?***
    – Possible Responses:
        i. Michael Vick.
        ii. Tiger Woods.
        iii. Brett Favre.
        iv. Terrell Owen.
        v. Lindsay Lohan.

6. ***What in the "game" gives all of us total control of our lives?***

    – Possible Responses:
        i. Choices!
        ii. Only you can make the final choices that will set the course your life will take.
        iii. People may give you advice but you will ultimately make the final choice.
        iv. You have total control of all of your choices.
        v. Therefore, you control your own destiny!

Key Points:

- Unwritten rules exist in every environment.
- It is possible to identify and understand the unwritten rules.
- Each person is in control of his/her destiny.
- Personal choices are up to the individual.

Chapter Ten Summary

The "Unwritten Rules" Of the Game

The unwritten rules are the elements that hold our system together. Like culture, they have been passed from generation to generation. There might be some new ones on this list you have not yet been exposed to, but most of the following rules you probably have already heard from your grandparents, parents, teachers, coaches and many other individuals who have tried to pass on to you the life experiences they have had, both bad and good.

The list is by no means complete but the ones listed will give you a solid base to build upon. The rules apply to human societies of today but I imagine that all began when humans first interacted with each other. The following are some of the important unwritten rules that we can now see in print.

Rules of the Game

- Life is a game. The game is about people and every-thing else is detail.
- Whoever is at the top of any pyramid has the right and the responsibility to make the rules.
- It is hard to go home again – except for a visit.
- Money is not the criterion for level acceptance.
- Never take a problem to someone without a solution.
- The game is about execution.
- Never wound your boss.
- You should work every day to make your boss look good.
- No one ever said that life (and your career) was going to be fair or easy.
- To move up, you must leave people behind.

- The game is about power. P.I.E. © is how you gain power.
- Positions in organizations correspond to our socio-economic levels.
- Once you have been sponsored to the next higher level – the finances needed to live there will be provided.
- Every opportunity has tradeoffs – there is no free lunch.
- Work smarter not harder.
- After cashing your paycheck – your company owes you nothing.
- Performance is a given.
- Performance gets you into the stadium – then the game begins.
- You are paid for performance – you are promoted based on someone's assessment of your potential.
- Contribute more than you cost.
- Take pride in your work.
- If anything is worth doing, it's worth doing right.

Skills of a Game Player

- Learn to listen.
- Choose wisely.
- When in doubt – trust your gut.
- No risk – no gain.
- Think outside the box.
- Be a team player.
- Never stop learning new things.
- Knowledge is power – education is the foundation of career success.

Emotional Control

- Keep your emotions under control.
- Count to ten before you speak.
- Don't burn your bridges.

- There is never a good reason to ever be rude.

Non-Verbal Messages

- Your actions speak louder than words.
- Talk is cheap –seeing is believing.
- A picture is worth a thousand words.
- Practice what you preach.

Change

- Change is constant.
- When you are through changing, you are through.
- You must challenge your personal comfort level in order to grow.
- "Letting go" is one of the most difficult skills to master.
- Embrace change.
- The only way change can occur is openness to feedback.
- No matter how much you change – you are still you – just a different you.
- Stay loose – be flexible.
- Personal change is like a language – you can become fluent in one to three years.

Self-Empowerment

- If you think you can, or if you think you can't – you're right. (***Henry Ford***)
- The pleasure you get from your life is equal to the attitude you put into it.
- All greatness is achieved while performing outside your comfort zone. (***Greg Arnold***)
- You can't build a reputation on what you are going to do. (***Henry Ford***)

- Nothing is too small to know, and nothing too big to attempt. (***William Van Home***)
- The difference between a successful person and others is not a lack of strength, not a lack of knowledge, but rather a lack of will. (***Vince Lombardi***)
- To avoid criticism do nothing, say nothing, be nothing. (***Elbert Hubbard***)
- You must have a high concept not of what you are doing, but of what you may do someday. Without that there's no point to working. (***Edgar Degas***)
- Unless you try something beyond what you have already accomplished, you will never grow! (***Ronald Olson***)
- Success is how high you bounce when you hit bottom. (***General George Patton***)
- A journey of a thousand miles must begin with a single step. (***Los – Tzu***)
- What lies behind us and before us are small matters compared to what lies within us. (***Ralph Waldo Emerson***)
- Even if you're on the right track, you'll get run over if you just sit there. (***Will Rogers***)
- It is hard to fail, but it is worse never to have tried to succeed. (***Theodore Roosevelt***)
- I am a great believer in luck, the harder I work, the more of it I seem to have. (***Coleman Cox***)
- It's not whether you get knocked down, it's whether you get up again! (***Vince Lombardi***)
- We first make our habits, and then our habits make us. (***D. A. Benton***)
- Failing to plan is planning to fail. (***Allen Lakein***)
- Just do it!
- Life is not a destination, it is a journey. It's what you do along the way.
- Take time to smell the roses.

HAVE A GOOD GAME!